BE RICH!

The Science of
Getting What You Want

Robert Collier

BE RICH!

Being "The Law of Increase" As Used by the Prophets of Old

Here is a secret of riches and success that has been buried 1,900 years deep.

Since time began, mankind has been searching for this secret. It has been found and lost again — a score of times. The Ancients of all races have had some inkling of it, as is proven by the folktales and legends that have come down to us, like the story of Aladdin and his wonderful lamp, or Ali Baba and his "Open Sesame" to the treasure trove.

Every nation has such legends. Every nation has had its Wise Men, its men of genius and vision who glimpsed the truth that is buried in these old folktales and who understood at least something of how it works.

But it remains for us to re-discover this secret in its entirety and then to show, clearly, step by step, how we might use it to bring us anything of good we might desire.

For make no mistake about it. Seeming miracles in the world are divinely NATURAL. Instead of being departures from natural law, they are demonstrations of what the law
will do for you if you understand how to use it!

God does not deal in exceptions. As one put it: "Miracles are not contrary to Nature, but only contrary to what we know about Nature."

Every force in Nature works along definite, logical lines, in accord with certain principles. These forces will work for anyone who possesses the key to their use, just as Aladdin's fabled Genie would respond to the call of anyone who rubbed the magic lamp.

They can be neglected and allowed to lie idle; they can be used for good or evil; but the laws themselves do not change. It is merely the methods of using them that change.

An aeroplane or an automobile would have seemed as great a miracle to the people of yesterday as the curing of a leper. Sending sound waves through the ether, to be picked up by a little box called a radio, would have been as wonderful to our fathers as is the sending of our voice over a beam of light to us today. Yet there is nothing super-natural about either of these.

The forces of Nature have always been there, ready for our use. It is our understanding of them that has changed, our knowledge of how to USE them.

Man in ancient times looked upon the lightning as the wrath of God, just as many deeply religious people look upon poverty and sickness and calamities today in the same way, as visitations of God. Yet man has learned to harness the lightning and make it serve him.
The laws governing electricity were there all the time, waiting only for the understanding of someone wise enough to show us how to put them to good use.

Just so, the power to BE and HAVE what you want is right here, needing only for you to learn how it works.

When you want more of the good things of life, when happiness or success or riches seem to elude you, there is a definite formula for you to use.

Go back over any of the miracles of increase in the Bible and see if they are not all miracles of EXPANSION. And what is expansion? It is increasing, spreading out, multiplying, is it not?

How did Elijah make the oil and meal last, so that one measure of oil and a little meal fed him and the widow and her soon for an indefinite period? How did Elisha increase the pot of oil for that other widow who came to him to saver her son from bondage, so that she had enough to

11

fill all the vessels she could borrow from her neighbors? By EXPANDING them, did they not? And how can you expand things? We know of only two methods:

1 By PRESSURE from within.
2 By HEAT.

If you want to expand something elastic, you can blow air or liquid into it and thus force it up under pressure, or you can push it out with your hands. But that sort of expansion lasts only as long as the pressure is applied.

To produce INCREASE, expansion must come from within the object itself, just as it comes from within every seed that grows. Such expansion comes only from HEAT. To expand water, for instance, you heat it until it becomes steam, and from that expanded vapor, you can get power to do greater work that thousands of men or hundreds of horses could do. If you want to expand metal, you bring it to a white heat, and while in that state, you can make of it anything your skill can contrive. If you want to expand coal, and draw from it the rich gases and coal tar and dyes and other derivatives hidden under its hard exterior, you have only to heat it. If you want to expand a seed of corn or wheat or

any fruit or vegetable, and have it grow and bring forth fruit and multiply, you must plant and water it so it will heat and burst its shell and send its shoots upward.

In short, the one prerequisite to the expansion of almost any element from within seems to be HEAT. But how can we use heat to expand our riches? Should we then throw everything into the fire and hope to get our increase from the flames? By no means.

Certainly that was not the way the Prophets did it. They used heat, but it was a different kind of heat. It was the heat of LOVE, of PRAISE and BLESSING, fanned by the breath of FAITH.

You who have worked with people especially with children or simple-minded folk know the effects of praise. Children expand under it. They do things they would otherwise find impossible. It seems to increase their energy. Certainly it taps wellsprings that are ordinarily closed to them.

The same is true in the handling of people. A famous Sales Manager was having difficulty with his men. Their sales had slumped, and all his "prep" talks, his urgings, his threats, had failed to bring them up again. He put up a large electric sign in the main corridor of his building, where everyone who came through would see it: "The salesman whose work has been most outstanding this week is..."

Immediately the sales jumped, and from that week on he never had to worry about a slump again.

How does this apply to inanimate things? The answer is that there are no inanimate things. Science today shows us that everything is full of life. Inside the apparently inert lump of lead or iron are tiny atoms of whirling energy, dashing here and there, bounding and rebounding and circling around like miniature solar systems, with a rapidity to which the speed of an aeroplane is as nothing. The mass as a mass may be quiet, but inside is boundless energy.

Where there is ceaseless energy, there is Life. Where movement is orderly and seemingly in accord with a well-laid plan, there is bound to be Intelligence. And where there is Intelligence, there must be RESPONSIVENESS.

It is this Responsiveness on the part of everything in life that makes it possible for you to prove the truth of the Scriptural promise that man should have DOMINION over the earth and over everything upon or under the earth.

How can you exercise that domination? Not by force. Not even by prayer. But by PRAISE!

As Charles Fillmore puts it "There is an inherent law of mind that we INCREASE whatever we PRAISE. The whole of creation responds to praise, and is glad. Animal trainers pet and reward their charges with delicacies for acts of obedience; children glow with joy and gladness when they are praised. Even vegetation grows better for those who love it. We can praise our own ability, and the very brain cells will expand and increase in capacity and intelligence, when we speak words of encouragement and appreciation to them."

God gave you dominion over the earth. Everything is your servant, but remember it is said in the Scriptures that God brought every beast and fowl to Adam, to see what he would call them. You are like Adam in this, that you can give to everything and everybody you come in contact with the name you like. You can call them good or bad. And whatever you call them, that is what they will be to you good servants or evil ones.

You can praise or curse them, and as you do, so will they be to you.

The Law of Increase

There is one unfailing Law of Increase "Whatever is praised and blessed, MULTIPLIES." Count your blessings and they increase. If you are in need of supply, start in now to praise every small piece of money that come to you, blessing it is a symbol of God's abundance and love. You will be surprised how soon that small piece will increase to

many pieces. Take God into your business. Bless your store, your cash register, every one that works for you, each customer that comes in. If you are working for someone else and want a better job or more pay, start by BLESSING and being THANKFUL for what you have. Bless the work you are doing, be thankful for every opportunity it gives you to acquire greater skill or ability or to serve others. Bless the money you earn, no matter how little it may be. Be so thankful to God for it that you can give a small "Thank offering" from it to someone in greater need than yourself.

Suppose the Boss does seem unappreciative and hard. Bless him just the same. Be thankful, for the opportunity to SERVE faithfully, no matter how small the immediate reward may seem to be. Give your best, give it cheerfully, gladly, thankfully, and you
will be amazed how quickly the INCREASE will come to you, not necessarily from your immediate boss, but from the Big Boss over all.

I remember reading a letter from a woman in the drought belt in which she said that they, unlike most of their neighbors, had an abundant supply of water, and excellent crops. "When my husband plows a field," she writes, "I ask God to bless each furrow. Each seed that goes into the seeder is blessed, and the realization held that it will produce abundantly according to His righteous law. Our neighbors marveled at the abundance of hay that we cut this year. The hay was sold before the third cutting was put up."

"Each day, in silence, I put the ranch 'Lovingly in the hands of the Father.' I ask God to bless everybody that comes in contact with the ranch."

Few realize the power of praise and blessing. Praise may be called the great liberator. Praise always magnifies. When we praise God and then look about us and praise His invisible presence in all that we see, we find that the good is so magnified that much becomes evident that we ordinarily fail to see.

Go back over the Bible and see how often you are adjured to "Praise the Lord and be thankful, that THEN shall the earth yield be increased."

Probably no life chronicled in the Scriptures was more beset with trials and danger than that of King David. And what was his remedy? What brought him through all tribulations to power and riches? Just read the Psalms.

"If anyone could tell you the shortest, surest way to all happiness and all perfection," wrote William Law, "he must tell you to make it a rule to yourself to thank and praise God for everything that happens to you. For it is certain that whatever seeming calamity happens to you, if you thank and praise God for it, you turn it into a blessing. Could you therefore work miracles, you could not do more for yourself than by this thankful spirit; for it turns all that it touches into happiness."

How then can YOU increase your supply? How can you get more of riches and happiness and every good thing of life? In the same way as the Wise Men and the Prophets of old. By EXPANDING what you have! And the way to expand is through love, through praise and thanksgiving.

Throughout the Bible we are told — WITH THANKSGIVING let your request be made known unto God. Again and again the root of inspiration and attainment is stressed: Rejoice, be glad, praise, give thanks!

One of the startling facts of modern science is that this universe is not a finished product. Creation is going on all around us — new worlds being formed, cosmic energy taking shape in a million different molds. But a far more startling fact to most of us is that WE ARE CREATORS, and that we can form today the world we personally shall be living tomorrow.

People blame their environment, their education, their opportunities, their luck, for their condition. They are wrong. There is one person to blame — and only one — THEMSELVES. They are today the result of their thoughts of yesterday and the many yesterdays that preceded it. They are forming today the mold for what they will be in the years to come.

For there is no such thing as failure. Whether you are poor or sickly, or rich and strong, you have succeeded in one thing. You have compressed the cosmic energy about you into the mold that you held before the mind's eye of your inner self. You have named the forces that worked with you "good" or "bad," and as you named them, so have they been to you as servant — Good or Evil.

But there is a happy ending. You don't need to leave things as they are. If you don't like the present results, you can rename those servants. You can bless and praise the good, no matter how tiny it may seem, and by your praise and blessing, you can expand it a thousand-fold.

Perhaps this may be easier to believe if you remember that it is the way all of

Nature works. Take the mineral kingdom: A group of cells shows "cohesion" or the ability to stick together. Why? Because all are of the same kind, the electronic life in them revolving at the same rate. In like manner, they possess the ability to repel any other kind

of cell that attempt to join the group, because the rate of motion in those other cells is different.

In the vegetable kingdom, the process of selection is greater. Each group of cells attracts to itself from its immediate environment all those cells that are exactly like those forming that particular plan, and it repels all other. Thus tomatoes and potatoes and beans and a dozen other vegetables can all grow side by side, yet remain entirely separate and distinct in their organisms. No part of the potato will be attracted by or absorbed into the tomato, or vice versa. Each uses its selective properties to remain true to type.

Like Attracts Like

It all goes back to the electrons and protons of which each individual cell whether mineral, animal or vegetable is made. Everything in Nature starts with this. A single electron is touched in just the right way to start it revolving on its axis. Its awakening affects other particles of a like nature, drawing them to it, setting them in motion like-wise.

Each electron is a small universe in itself, with revolving particles turning about a common center with the same motion and at the same relative distances that the earth and planets revolve around the sun.

It is the RATE of movement that variation occurs. Those groups that have higher rate of movement produce the higher forms of life. The moment that the

rate of movement changes, form and color are changed, and in the case of complicated organisms like the human body, the change in the rate of movement of any part of the body may readily
affect the harmony of the whole, for with differences in rotation, the faster units have a tendency to break away from and throw off the slower.

Something of this kind is going on in the body all the time. Older cells slow down, break away and are thrown out. That is how a dog follows the scent of its master by the trail of old, discarded cells that he is continually throwing off. It is only when we fail to throw
off the inharmonious cells that disease gets a foothold and we sicken or die.

Remember this: Starting with the individual cell, we attract to us only those elements that are identical in quality and character with ourselves, and that are revolving at the same rate of speed. Our selective ability is such that we are able to pick such material as

will preserve our quality and identity. This is true of our bodies, of our circumstances, of our environment. Like attracts like.

If we are not satisfied with ourselves as we are, if we want a healthier body, more attractive friends, greater riches, and success, we must start at the core within ourselves!

And that core lies in our thoughts. Thought can speed up or slow down the rate of motion of the whole body. Thought can retard certain organs, and thus cause inharmony throughout the whole body. Thoughts of anger, fear, worry, envy, hatred or discouragement can create such inharmony as to bring about cancerous growths in the body as well as disaster in one's affairs. You can cut out such growths with a surgeon's knife, and thus help the body organism to throw off the inharmonious elements, but an easier way, a better way, is to bring the body back into harmony, bring the entire organism into tune.

In Tune With the Infinite

The first essential to putting yourself in harmony with the Infinite Good about you is to relax, to take off the brakes. For what is worry or fear or discouragement but a brake on your thinking and the proper functioning of your organs, a slowing down of your entire rate of activity?

It is said that the Devil once held a sale of all the tools of his trade. Everything was displayed — his keen-edged daggers of jealousy, his sledgehammer of anger, his bow of greed, his arrows of lust and covetousness, his weapons of vanity and fear and envy and pride. And under each was its price.

But in the place of honor, framed and set apart from all the rest was a small wedge, dented and marked with use. The name of this wedge was "Discouragement," and the price set upon it was higher than all the other tools combined.

Asked the reason for this amazing difference, the Devil explained — "it is because this is the one tool I can use when all others fail. Let me get that little wedge into a man's consciousness, and it opens the way for everything else. That wedge has opened more doors to me than all my other weapons combined."

Few things will slow down your rate of activity as much as Discouragement. Few offer greater resistance to the good that is trying to manifest through you.

You remember Ohm's Law in electricity, $C = E$ divided by R. C is the amount of electrical energy to be delivered at the point of use. E is the amount available from the powerhouse. R represents the resistance offered by all the things through which the current must flow.

If there were no resistance, the full amount of current generated by E would be delivered. But there is always some resistance. Even the best conductor offers a little, and you can't deliver current without a conductor. So the amount actually delivered depends upon the power available, divided by the resistance.

All the energy of the universe is around you. You can have anything of good you desire. But it must first go through you — and you won't let it. You put up more resistance to good than all the non-conductors that ever interfered with an electrical circuit.

You can't believe that good is so easily available. You feel that it can come to you only after hard struggle, and disappointments and pain. You insist upon putting these non-conductors in its path. You add worries and fears and hates and envies, so that by the time the good reaches you, its current is so weak that there is little left.

Like attracts like. Hate brings hate, and all the ills that follow in its wake. Envy and fear and worry attract discord and disease. If you want health, happiness, in your life, if you are seeking riches and success, attune your thoughts to these. BLESS the circumstances that surround you. Bless and praise those who come in contact with you. Bless even the difficulties you meet, for by blessing them, you can change them from discordant conditions to favorable ones, you can speed up their rate of activity to where they will bring you good instead of evil.

It is only lack of RESPONSIVENESS to good that produces the lacks in your life. Good works on the plane of EXPANSION. Good revolves at a high rate of activity. You can key your activity to the same rate by an expectant confident state of mind. You can bring all your surroundings and circumstances up to that same level by BLESSING them, PRAISING the good in them.

Remember, the basic magnet lies in your own thoughts. Upon the quality and activity of that magnet depend the good or evil that will be drawn to you. You are the Master of your fate. You are the architect who determines the materials that are to be used in making your life and your circumstances. You have the power of SELECTIVITY.

How, then, shall we order our lives, to the end that we may have the good things we seek — riches and happiness, health and success?

The Nucleus

Remember, everything in this universe must start with a nucleus. A single electron is touched in the right way to start revolving on its axis. The magnetism engendered by it draws to it other particles of a like nature, setting them in motion likewise. With that as a nucleus, it can grow and multiply indefinitely, as long as its rate of motion continues. It is only when something slows it down that it disintegrates and dies.

How can you start such a nucleus? With an IDEA, backed by earnest desire and faith.

Suppose you want to build a business of your own, for instance. I'll tell you how one man of my acquaintance did it. When Bruce Haughton decided to start an automotive business in Jacksonville, FL., he had only $23.00 to his name. With $14.40 of his capital, he bought some tools. Then he rented the 2-car garage in the back yard of the house where he had secured a room and set up his sign!

He did not depend upon the sign, however, to bring in business. He figured that he was the only one who could do that. So he called upon a number of professional men and told them of the personal service he could give their cars, which they could not get elsewhere. In odd moments during the next few weeks, he continued those calls. Thereafter he used letters and postcards to tell more people about his distinctive service.

At the end of the first thirty days, he had a net return from his investment of money, work and brains of $476.80, with an overhead expense of only $50.00. That was in the spring. By June, he found that he needed bigger quarters, for 591 regular customers were already coming to his "Back Yard Garage" for service they could not buy elsewhere.

In February of the following year, he had to move again, this time to a corner in one of the best parts of the city. A year later, he moved a third time closer by five blocks to the business section, within easy reach of the big office building where the larger part of his clientele was located — and ten times as big as his last place!

Not only that, but he started a Motor Club that soon had fifty branches all over Florida and Georgia. In these garages, his products were sold, his name became known, his service talked about.

And all on a capital of $23.00! On that, and an idea, and work, and a thorough belief in his ability to render a better service than anyone else could give!

But perhaps you will say — "He had special skill. He was a good auto mechanic. I have no particular skill or ability. What am I to do?"

Find some way of serving people better or more economically than it is now being done. Then learn HOW to do it, even though it means putting off the carrying out of your idea for months or years. With all the free night schools and public libraries of today, there is no excuse for not being able to learn anything you want to know.

Here is the way a friend of mine got out of the $25.00 a week class and into a

highly profitable business. He had an idea that women's clothes cost entirely too much, that if he could bring down the price a third, he could get the trade of many girls working in offices and stores, girls who must look well dressed but have not too much money to spend
on clothes.

So what did he do? He took a low-paid job as assistant to a resident buyer; really not much more than a messenger boy. But it took him into all the manufactures' workshops. It made him acquainted with everyone who made the kind of dresses he was interested in. It gave him an insight into wholesale prices and methods of buying. When he was ready,
he raised a little money through family and friends and opened a small upstairs office.

Then he made daily rounds of the manufactures, picking up a discontinued model here, a job lot there, a few specials somewhere else — all at prices far below the usual wholesale figures.

As soon as he felt that he had enough to start with, he sent letters to lists of women working in nearby offices and shops, telling them of the unusual bargains he was able to offer and the reason for them. The result? Before the year was out, he had a profitable, growing business.

First the nucleus, the idea. Then something to start it into action, to make it revolve and draw to itself everything it needs for growth.

What is it YOU want — a home, a job, a business, money or health? You can get any or all of them, if you have the initiative to start something, the faith to carry on in the face of all obstacles.

For don't forget this: No matter how good your start, your nucleus will not carry on by itself. It needs faith to keep it moving. It needs the urge of BELIEF to speed it up and give it the magnetic power to draw to itself the elements it needs for growth and strength, when obstacles get in its way and threaten to slow it down or stop it.

Why is it that few businesses outlast their founder? Because the founder lacks the necessary faith and determination to keep the nucleus whirling. Faith is the motive power without which no business can run, without which any nucleus will speedily slow down and lose all its magnetic force.

You want a home, let us say, but you lack the money to buy the kind you would like. Forget money for the moment. That is not the most important part. Instead, picture on paper the exact type of home you are longing for. Cut from magazines illustrations showing just what you want in a home — the type of architecture, the construction, the grounds, the different rooms, even the furnishings. Put your Dream House on paper.

That is your nucleus. Now start it whirling. Now give it life. How? By doing something towards bringing that home into materialization.

One woman got a board and nails, and started to make a kitchen shelf. Another went to the 5 & 10¢ store each day and bought some item for the kitchen.

Do something to show your faith. Do something to start your nucleus into action, and continue to do little things. Not only that, but every time you look upon the picture of your Dream Home, admire it, be thankful for it, and BELIEVE in it. "As your faith is, so shall it be unto you," for it is your faith that provides the propelling force to your nucleus and gives it power to draw to it every element needed for its growth and fruition.

Suppose you want to sell something. Perhaps it is an idea you have for improving the business and you want to convince the boss of its value. Perhaps it is a car or an insurance policy or some other product that you feel some particular prospect should buy. Perhaps you want to sell some girl the idea that you would make her the ideal husband. How shall you go about it?

By selling YOURSELF first! Every sale, of whatever kind, must be made in your own mind first. Stand in front of a mirror and talk to the image reflected there. Sell him! Give him every argument you would give your prospect. Then look him in the eye and ask him "Do you believe this?" If he does not, depend upon it, your prospect will not. But if
you can truly convince that man in the mirror, if you can look him in the eye and talk to him honestly, sincerely, convincingly, and have him nod in agreement with you, then believe me, you can sell anyone.

You have put life into your nucleus. You have started it whirling. You can call on your prospect, whoever he is, with the confident assurance that your sale is made. It may not be accomplished on the first visit. It may not be done on the second. Your nucleus may have to draw to itself other elements to complete the transaction, but if you can hold the faith, if you can keep the man in the mirror sold, your success is assured.

Napoleon Hill wrote "There is only one unfailing law of success in business; it is BELIEF!"

But how about health? What if you are ailing, weak, run down, and sickly? More than 2,000 years ago, the Prophet Joel answered that question "Let the weak say, I am strong!" Shakespeare told us much the same when he said "Assume a virtue if you have it not."

What is sickness? A slowing down of the vital processes, is it not? Every cell in your body is just a whirling bit of energy. Any that slow down are thrown off, excreted.

But when the whole system slows down, you don't throw off the waste matter, you don't get rid of the poisons. The result? Aches and pains and a general feeling of lassitude and illness. What better remedy could there be than speeding up your rate of motion, re-energizing all your cells and helping them to throw off all the elements that tend to slow you down.

You CAN do it. You know that martial music will reanimate soldiers ready to drop with fatigue. You know that fragrant perfumes brighten you, that a sunshiny morning gives you more life and pep. Why is it that inmates of insane asylums are more easily controlled if given plenty

49

of sunshine? Why are children better behaved, why do YOU

feel better, think better, act better when you have the benefit of the sun's rays? Why is there so much truth in the old, Italian proverb "Where the sun goes, the doctor goes not?"

Because sunshine not only speeds up the rate of motion of your cells, but as one authority puts it — "Sunlight is actually a food to the human body, stimulates growth, promotes the healthy functioning of blood and nerves."

Cheerful affirmations, convincingly given, have the same stimulating effect. Thirty years ago, Emile Coue electrified the world with his cures of all manner of disease. "Nobody ought to be sick!" he proclaimed, and proceeded to prove it by curing hundreds who came to him after doctors had failed to relieve them. Not only that, but he showed how the same methods could be used to cure one's affairs, to bring riches instead of debts, success instead of drudgery.

What was back of his success? A law as old as the hills, a law that has been known to psychologists for years — the law that the subconscious mind accepts as TRUE anything that is repeated to it convincingly and often. And once it has accepted such a statement as true, it proceeds to do everything in its power to MAKE IT TRUE!

You ask a friend how he is, and he carelessly answers — "I am sick, I am poor, I am unlucky," never stopping to think that by those very words he is fastening misfortune upon himself, suggesting to his subconscious mind that it proceed on the assumption that he IS sick or poor or weak or unfortunate.

FAITH will make you whole. But how, you may ask, can you work up such faith? There are two ways.

The first is through affirmations — CLAIMING the thing you want, telling your subconscious that you HAVE it, and keep on telling it in such convincing tones that it finally accepts the statement as fact and proceeds to bring it into being. That was Coue's way. His "Every day in every way I am getting better and better" or "richer and richer" helped many people.

But if you want the best results, add this second factor: Stand in front of your mirror, look your reflection in the eye and talk to it as you would if you were a salesman, and upon you selling the man in the mirror depended everything important in your life. For it does!

If it is health you want, use some such affirmation as this: "I am energy. I am strength. I am power. I am filled and thrilled with omnipotent life. The vitality of God permeates every fiber of my being. I am well and whole in every part of my body. The grace and poise of God enfolds me. O Living Father, this is thy holy temple. Thou are making it a perfect dwelling place from which shall radiate thy healing love and wisdom to all mankind. Father, thou art glorifying me that I also may glorify thee."

Tell him that and BELIEVE it! When you can convince him that you do believe it, you will be well.

Here is another potent affirmation: "Life abundant quickens me now. Love all-powerful heals me. God's strong, pure life is now active in and through every cell in my body.

His perfect image of my every organ is now vitalized in me in perfect form. Every cell in my body is vitalized and restored. I have come to Him and I am healed."

Money, success, happiness, can all be won in the same way. They all start with a nucleus, an idea, an ambition, a desire. They all require you to DO something to start that nucleus revolving on its axis and drawing to itself the elements necessary for its growth and successful completion. They all need faith to speed up the rate of motion and keep

the nucleus growing.

Faith is the great impelling force. "If thou canst believe, all things are possible unto you."

There Is Magic In Believing

Professor William James of Harvard, the greatest psychologist America has known, declared that belief is oftentimes the only thing that can assure the successful conclusion of doubtful undertaking. Man's faith acts upon all the forces about him to bring into being the results that he images and believes in.

You can readily understand that when you realize that it is only faith that can keep the nucleus of an idea or a business going, if obstacles beset its path. You must hold to your image of the completed undertaking. You must see it successful in your mind's eye. You must BELIEVE in it.

How did God create the heavens and the earth and everything that in them is? You read in the Scriptures that God made "Every plant of the field before it was on the earth, and every herb of the field before it grew!" How did he do it? In the same way that He made man. "In his image He created Him." He "Imaged" man in His mind.

"In the beginning was the word." What is a word? A mental image, is it not? "In the beginning was the mental image." That is the way everything in it is created right down to this day, from the building of a house to the laying of a transcontinental railway.

Do you remember the story of Jacob? He agreed to serve his Uncle Laban seven years to win the hand of Laban's daughter Rachel in marriage, but through the guile of Laban, Jacob had to serve a second seven years. Even then, Laban begged him to tarry longer, and agreed to pay him as wages "all the speckled and spotted cattle, and all the brown cattle among the sheep, and the speckled and the spotted among the goats." Since Laban first removed from the herds all cattle of this kind, the chances of Jacob's getting rich on the speckled offspring of solid-colored cattle seemed poor indeed.

But Jacob evidently knew the power of "imaging," of visualization, for what did he do?

"And Jacob took him rods which he had piled before the flocks in the gutters of the watering troughs when the flocks came to drink, that they should conceive when they came to drink." "And the flocks conceived before the rods, and brought forth

ringstaked, speckled and spotted."

"And Jacob did separate the lambs, and set the faces of the flocks toward the ring staked and all the brown in the flock of Laban; and he put his own flocks by themselves, and put their not unto Laban's cattle."

"And it came to pass, whensoever the strong cattle did conceive, that Jacob laid the rods before the eyes of the cattle in the gutters that they might conceive among the rods."

"But when the cattle were feeble, he put them not in; so the feeble were Laban's and the stronger Jacob's."

"And the man increased exceedingly, and had much cattle, and maidservants and menservants and camels and asses."

In everything God created, the "Word" or mental image came first, then the material form. And that is the way it is with you.

Get the right image in your mind, put your faith in it and you can bring it into being.

You control your destiny, your fortune, your happiness, to the exact extent to which you can think them out, visualize them, see them as already yours. Allow no vagrant thought of fear or worry to mar their completion and beauty. The quality of your thought is the measure of your power.

"The source and center of all man's creative power," writes Glenn Clark, "the power that above all others lifts him above the level of brute creation and that gives him dominion, is his power of making images, or the power of the imagination."

There is a very real law of cause and effect which makes the dream of the dreamer come true. It is the law of visualization and belief — the law that calls into being in this outer world everything that we truly believe to be real in the inner world.

Imagination pictures the thing you desire. Action starts your nucleus whirling and growing. Belief gives magnetic power to it, enabling it to attract to itself every element it needs to bring it into reality. It reaches beyond the thing that is, into the conception of what can be.

Imagination gives you the picture. Belief gives you the power to make that picture your own.

Make your mental image clear enough —
picture it vividly enough — give it action
and belief and all the powers of the
universe will join to help you bring it into
being.

That law holds true of everything in life.
There is nothing you can rightfully desire
that cannot be brought into being through
visualization, action and belief.

The keynote of successful visualization is
this; See things as you would have them
be instead of as they are. Close your eyes
and make clear mental pictures. Make
them look and act just as they would if
they were real. In short, daydream
purposefully. Then put foundations under
your dreams with your belief.

As James Allen put it: "Dream lofty dreams, and as you dream, so shall you become. Your vision is the promise of what you shall one day be. Your ideal is the prophecy of what you shall at last unveil."

The mental image is what counts, be it for good or ill. It is a devastating or beneficent force, just as you choose to make it. To paraphrase Thackeray — "The world is a looking glass, and gives back to every man the reflection of his own thought."

Every condition, every experience of life is the result of our mental attitude. We can do only what we think we can do. We can be only what we think we can be. We can have only what we think we can have. What we do, what we are, what we have, all depend upon what we think. We can never express anything that we do not first have in mind.

The secret of all power, all success, all riches, is in first thinking powerful thoughts, successful thoughts, thoughts of wealth and supply. We must build them in our minds first. "Could we rightly comprehend the mind of man," wrote Paracelsus, "nothing would be impossible to us upon the earth." And Buddha told his followers — "All that we are is the result of what we have thought." And thought is subject wholly to the control of mind. Its direction rests with us. So learn to control your thought. Learn to image upon your mind only things you want to see reflected in your outer circumstances. Our achievements of today are but the sum of our thoughts of yesterday.

Remember, you can have anything you want if you want it badly enough. You can be anything you want to be, have anything you desire, accomplish anything you set out to accomplish — if you will hold to that desire with singleness of purpose; if you will understand and believe in your own powers to accomplish.

Just as the first law of gain is desire, so the formula of success is belief. Believe that you have it — see it as an existent fact — and anything you can rightly wish for is yours. Belief is the substance of things hoped for, the evidence of things not seen.

It is your BELIEF in yourself that counts. It is the consciousness of dominant power within you that makes all things attainable. You can do anything you think you can. This knowledge is literally the gift of the gods, for through it you can solve every human problem. It is the open door to all good that you desire.

But do not let doubts or fears creep in. As Baudouin said: "To be ambitious for wealth and yet always expecting to be poor; to be always doubting your ability to get what you long for, is like trying to reach east by traveling west. There is no philosophy which will help a man to succeed when he is always doubting his ability to do so, and thus attracting failure.

"You will go in the direction in which you face. There is a saying that every time the sheep bleats, it loses a mouthful of hay. Every time you allow yourself to complain of your lot, to say 'I am poor; I can never do what others do; I shall never be rich; I have not the ability that others have;' you are laying up so much trouble for yourself.

"No matter how hard you may work for success, if your thought is saturated with the fear of failure, it will kill your efforts, neutralize your endeavors, and make success impossible."

Learn to control your thought. Learn to image upon your mind only the things you want to see reflected in your outer circumstances. Your achievements of today are but the sum of your thoughts and beliefs of yesterday. Your chances of success in any undertaking can always be measured by your belief in yourself.

Suppose your surroundings are discouraging. Just bear in mind that your real environment is within you. All the factors that make for success or failure are in your inner world. YOU make that inner world — and through it your outer world. You can choose the material from which to build it. The richness of life is within you. No one has failed as long as he can begin again.

So start now to do the things you feel you have it in you to do. Ask permission of no man. Your belief that you can do the thing gives your thought-force their power. Fortune waits upon you. Seize her boldly, hold her and she is yours. She belongs rightfully to you.

The men who have made their mark in this world all had one trait in common — they believed in themselves.

So what do you want most from life? Whatever it is, you can have it — if you can believe in it — if you can see in it in your mind's eye as yours. You must be able to hold it in your thought, visualize it, see yourself having it. You must make your model clear-cut and distinct.

1. Remember, the first thing necessary is a sincere desire, concentrating your thought on one thing with singleness of purpose.

2. The second is visualization, seeing yourself doing it, imaging the object in the same way that God first imaged everything He created.

3. The third essential is to take whatever action is necessary to start your nucleus revolving and growing.

4. Next is faith, believing that you HAVE the thing you want, affirming constantly to your image in the mirror that you ARE rich or successful or healthy or happy. Not that you are going to be, mind you but that you ARE!

5. And the last is gratitude, gratitude for this thing that you have received, for the power that enabled you to create it, for all the gifts that Mind has given you in such profusion. Thank God that you HAVE received.

The Law of Attraction

What is the greatest evil in the world today? What causes more misery, more sin, than all other vices combined? What is the worst enemy of morality and peace and happiness that mankind knows?

POVERTY!

Poverty is responsible for most commercialized vice. Poverty fills our prisons with thieves and murderers. Poverty causes most disease. Poverty is back of nine-tenths of the unhappiness and misery in the world. It drives men to drink and to suicide, women to that and more. It makes people do things that otherwise they would look upon with loathing.

Poverty is a vice. It is true that some of the churches still catalog it among the virtues, but that is a relic of the old feudal days when the few had all the riches and the many were left to wallow in misery. To keep the masses from revolution, it was necessary to teach them that God ordered it thus that there was not enough of the good things of life to go around, so that the many must suffer here that the few might enjoy, but it would all be made right in the next world.

We know now that this was mere "pap" to keep the masses quiet. We know that, for every individual to whom poverty has acted as a goad to high achievement, a thousand others have spent lives of squalor and misery. We know that the old idea that there was not enough to go around was just as foolish as that God would pick a particular class of "nobility" and give them everything good while letting the common people starve.

There are more riches in this old earth than mankind can ever exhaust. There is more power in the atom alone than man can ever use. There are unlimited resources of food and riches and comfort as yet undreamed of by man.

Why then do so many live in squalor, even in this richest country in the world? Why do millions die of famine in India and China? For the same reason that a party of explorers, driven by a west wind from the Amazon River far out to sea, and drifting in a river of fresh water, almost perished of thirst!

In much the same way, millions of human beings, living in a world of plenty, perish of want.

God is not partial to a fortunate few. He does not give to them and let the rest starve. He gives freely to all!

But there are certain laws governing these riches of His. There are rules that must be complied with. And until you learn the rules, you are like Ali Baba without the magic "Open, Sesame!" to open the doors of the treasure trove.

You have heard of Einstein's "Law of Relativity." And you probably wondered at times why such a to-do should be made over an obscure scientific law that could have no bearing, as far as you could see, upon everyday life.

But do you know that Einstein's theory is as important to you as any law in the land? For on what is his theory based?

1st, that there is only one material in the Universe.

2nd, and this is the part with a direct bearing upon you — that there is only one fundamental Law of the Universe. That law is the Law of Attraction.

To put it in ordinary, everyday language, Einstein's Law of the Universe means that you must either be an Attracter, drawing things to you, or else be willing to sit back and see everything that is yours attracted to some stronger personality.

Does that seem unjust? If so, it is still the way that all of Nature works. Take any seed of plant life. Take an acorn, for instance. You put it in the ground — plant it. What happens? It first gives of all the elements it has within itself to put forth a shoot, which in turn shall draw from the sun and the air the elements that they have to give; and at the same time, it puts out roots to draw from the earth the moisture and other elements it needs for growth. Its top reaches upward to the sun and air, its roots burrow deeply into the ground for moisture and nourishment. Always it is reaching out. Always it is creating a vacuum, using up all the materials it has on hand, drawing to itself from all about every element it needs for growth.

Time passes. The oak tree stops growing. What happens? In that moment, its attractive power ceases. Can it then live on the elements it has drawn to itself and made a part of itself through all those years? No, indeed! The moment growth stops, disintegration starts. Its component elements begin to feel the pull of the growing plants around them.

First the moisture drains out of the tree. Then the leaves fall, the bark peels off — finally the great trunk crashes down, to decay and form soil to nourish the growing plants around. Soon of the noble oak, nothing is left but the enriched soil and the well-nourished plants that have sprung from it.

The Fundamental Law of the Universe is that you must integrate or disintegrate. You must grow — or feed others who are growing. There is no standing still. You must speed up your rate of motion until you are attracting to yourself all the unused forces about you, or you must give your own to help build some other man's success.

"To him that hath, shall be given." To him that is using his attractive powers, shall be given everything he needs for growth and fruition.

"From him that hath not, shall be taken away even that which he hath." The penalty for not using your attractive powers is the loss of them. You are de-magnetized. And like a dead magnet surrounded by live ones, you must be content to see everything you have drawn to yourself taken by them, until eventually even you are absorbed by their resistless force.

That is the first and fundamental Law of the Universe. But how are you to become an Attracter? How are you to make your start? In the same way that it has been done from the beginning of time.

Go back to the first law of life. Go back to the beginning of things. You find Nature logical in all that she does. If you want to understand how she works, study her in her simplest, most elementary forms. The principle established there holds good throughout the universe. The methods there used are used by all created things, from the simplest to the most complicated.

How, for instance, did the earliest forms of cell life, either plant or animal, get their food? By absorbing it from the waters around them. How does every cell in your body, every cell in plant or tree or animal, get its food today? In exactly the same way, by absorbing it from the lymph or water surrounding it! Nature's methods do not change. She is logical in everything. She may build more complicated organisms, she may go in for immense size or strange combinations, but she uses the same principles throughout all of life.

Now, what is Nature's principle of Increase? From the beginning of time, it has been —
DIVIDE and GROW. That principle, like every other fundamental Law of Nature, is the same in all of life. It has remained unchanged since the first single-celled organism floated on the surface of the primordial sea. It is the fundamental Law of Increase.

Take the lowest form of cell life. How does it grow? It DIVIDES — each part grows back to its original size — then they in turn divide and grow again.

Take the highest form of cell life, MAN.
The same principle works in him in
exactly the same way in fact, it is the only
principle of growth that Nature knows!

How does this apply to your
circumstances, to the acquisition of
riches, to the winning of success? Look
up any miracle of increase in the Bible,
and what do you find?

First division; then increase. When the
widow of Zaraphath told Elijah she had
only a handful of meal and a little oil, he
bade her make from these a cake and give
it to him
— and after that, to make for herself and
her son. She did so, and it is written that
the barrel of meal wasted not; neither did
the oil fail.

When another widow came to Elisha to beg that he save her sons from bondage for debt, he asked her — "What hast thou in the house?" And when she answered — "Naught save a pot of oil," he bade her borrow vessels from the neighbors and pour out the oil into them. In other words, start the flow. And so long as she had vessels to receive it,

the oil kept flowing.

When Russell Conwell was building the famous Baptist Temple in Philadelphia, his congregation was poor and greatly in need of money. Through prayer and every other means known to man, Conwell was constantly trying to help his flock.

One Sunday it occurred to him that the old Jewish custom had been, when praying to God, to first make an offering of the finest lamb of the flock, or of some other much prized possession. Then, after freely giving to God, prayer was make for His good gifts.

So instead of first praying, and then taking up the collection, as was the custom, Conwell suggested that the collection be taken first and that all who had special favors to ask of the Creator should give freely as a "Thank Offering."

A few weeks afterwards, Conwell asked that those who had made offering on this occasion should tell their experiences. The results sounded unbelievable. One woman who had an overdue mortgage on her home found it necessary to call in a plumber the following week to repair a leak. In tearing up the boards, he uncovered a hiding place where her late father had hidden all his money — enough to pay off the mortgage and leave plenty over!

One man got a much-needed job. A servant some dresses she badly wanted. A student the chance to study for his chosen vocation. Literally dozens had their financial needs met. They had complied with the law. They had sown their seed — freely — and they reaped the harvest.

Many people will tell you "I don't see why God does not send me riches. I have prayed for them, and promised that if I get them, I will use them to do good."

God enters into no bargains with man. He gives you certain gifts to start, and upon the way you use these depends whether you get more. You've got to start with what you have. It's no use saying you have not enough to be worth starting with. You have a mind. You get ideas in abundance — ideas that might better the lot of those around you, ideas for service, ideas for making people happy, for improving conditions, for anything of good. Put them to work! Use them! ACT upon them! In your mind, they are no more than daydreams — Castles in the Air. Put foundations under them by DOING something to start them into action.

Remember, everything in this universe starts with a nucleus. It can be an idea, an ambition, or your Heart's Desire. But a nucleus of itself has no power. It cannot attract to itself even a single element. YOU have to set it in motion. YOU have to give it life. "Divide and grow!" Give it something of yours to get it started, whether it be money or
time or action or all of them. Start it whirling. Give it attractive power.

How can you do it? First, by starting something. If you want a particular job, for instance, a particular work or opportunity, start the wheels in motion that should bring it to you. If it requires special knowledge, study until you have that knowledge. If it requires influence, cultivate those who have that influence. Whatever it requires, do those things and while doing them, stand before your mirror each morning and night, and convince your image there that you HAVE what it takes to get it.

Speed up the rate of motion of your nucleus by your faith in yourself. See yourself in your mind's eye doing the things that will be required of you when you land the job. If it is possible to do so, act out the things that will be expected of you before your mirror. Never pass a mirror without looking your image in the eye and telling him you ARE a success, you ARE accomplishing whatever it is that you have in mind.

Remember always — first comes the mental image, then the fulfillment. Get that mental image clearly in mind, do something to start it into being, believe in it and the materialization will soon follow. But until you get it clearly in your own mind, you have a poor chance of putting it into the mind of anyone else.

"For anything that you want in life," writes Emmet Fox, "a healthy body, a satisfactory vacation, friends, opportunity, and above all the understanding of God, you must furnish a mental equivalent. Granted the mental equivalent, the thing must come to you." And what is the mental equivalent? What

but the image you hold in your mind's eye of the
things you want.

Thousands of books have been written on how to be successful, how to win your Heart's Desire, but here is the meat of all: Every nucleus has power to draw to itself anything it needs for growth and fruition, if started into action and speeded up by constant faith.

That knowledge should enable anyone to succeed. That knowledge is worth any price you may pay for it. It can enable you to overcome any handicap, to surmount any obstacle. It is literally the Gift of the Gods.

So start something — no matter on how small a scale. To begin, you know, is to be half done. Making a beginning starts your nucleus whirling, and that in turn affects everything about you of a like nature, drawing it to you, setting it in motion likewise.

A strong desire, backed by a firmly held purpose, is like a powerful magnet, drawing to it everything it needs for growth and fruition. But remember that the power of this magnet is dependent entirely upon your belief in it.

Perhaps you will recall the experiment made many years ago by Professor Henry of Princeton. He took an ordinary magnet of large size and with it lifted a few pounds of iron. Then he wrapped the magnet with wire charged from the current of a small battery.

Instead of only a few pounds, the magnet lifted 3,000 pounds of iron!

Your belief in yourself is like the current from that battery. It magnetizes you tenfold — even a hundredfold. It enables you to draw to you anything you need for success.

Working up this necessary belief may be difficult, but it is absolutely essential for without it you cannot succeed. Affirmation can be a great help, as suggested in the forgoing pages, and further study along these lines will help, too.

25 years ago, we wrote a set of little books called THE SECRET OF THE AGES, which explained in far greater detail the power that is in you and how to use it. Through the reading of these books, one man developed such a belief in himself and his mission in life that he

started a new religion that now numbers more than a hundred thousand members.

Through them, Lewis E. Sherbert of Reno learned to use the power that was in him to such good purpose that he wrote us a short time ago — "When I began reading THE SECRET OF THE AGES, I was a peddler earning perhaps $15 a week. Since then, thanks to Robert Collier, I have enjoyed many $25,000 years of prosperity."

Through these books, M. D. Couch found the inspiration that enabled him to start a new company which made him more that $100,000, where his previous income over a period of years had been only $7,500 a year.

There were hundreds more who wrote in similar vein, so that the *Commercial Reporter* said of them — "These little books have changed hundreds of lives from humdrum drudgery, business worry, and unsettlement, into sunshine and achievement."

Be Rich
The Science of getting
what you want

Idea	38
define	44
faith	69 - 70
	75
	78

11
24
34

We have Book Recommendations for you

Joseph Murphy: Neutralizing Negative
Suggestions
Download - Free Shipping!!!!

Joseph Murphy: The Unbelieveable Power
of Suggestion
Download - Free Shipping!!!!

The Power of Your Subconscious Mind by
Joseph Murphy
ABRIDGED - (Audio CD)

The Power of Your Subconscious Mind by
Joseph Murphy
MP3 [UNABRIDGED] (Audio CD)

Think and Grow Rich [MP3 AUDIO]
[UNABRIDGED]
by Napoleon Hill, Jason McCoy (Narrator)
(Audio CD - January 30, 2006)

As a Man Thinketh [UNABRIDGED]
by James Allen, Jason McCoy (Narrator)
(Audio CD - May 1, 2005)

Your Invisible Power: How to Attain Your
Desires by Letting Your Subconscious
Mind Work for You [MP3 AUDIO]
[UNABRIDGED]
by Genevieve Behrend, Jason McCoy
(Narrator) (Audio CD - February 9, 2006)

Thought Vibration or the Law of Attraction
in the Thought World [MP3 AUDIO]
[UNABRIDGED]
by William Walker Atkinson, Jason McCoy
(Narrator) (Audio CD - July 1, 2005)

BN Publishing

Improving People's Life

www.bnpublishing.com

98

BN Publishing

Improving People's Life

www.bnpublishing.com

BN Publishing

Improving People's Life

www.bnpublishing.com

CPSIA information can be obtained at www.ICGtesting.com
Printed in the USA
BVOW012143091011

273211BV00001B/58/A